CATHOLIC
PRAYERS AND PRACTICES

including
THE ORDER OF MASS

PETER M. ESPOSITO
President

JO ROTUNNO
Publisher

CREDITS AND ACKNOWLEDGMENTS

Copyright © 2012 by RCL Publishing LLC

Send all inquiries to:
RCL Benziger
8805 Governor's Hill Drive
Suite 400
Cincinnati, Ohio 45249

Toll Free 877-275-4725
Fax 800-688-8356
Visit us at **RCLBenziger.com**

978-0-7829-1619-5
(Catholic Prayers and Practices)

4th Printing
November 2013

Associate Publisher: Anne Battes
Cover and Page Design: Mary Wessel

ACKNOWLEDGMENTS

Excerpts are taken or adapted from the English translation of the *Roman Missal* © 2010 ICEL; the English translation of the Act of Contrition from *Rite of Penance* © 1974, ICEL; the English translation of *A Book of Prayers* © 1982, ICEL; *Catholic Household Blessings and Prayers* (revised edition) © 2007, United States Conference of Catholic Bishops, Washington, D.C. All rights reserved.

© 1994, Archdiocese of Chicago; Liturgy Training Publications, art by Martin Erspamer, OSB.

Dear Friends in Christ,

This small book, *Catholic Prayers and Practices* including The Order of Mass, contains traditional practices and prayers that unite us as Catholics. It is designed to support you in your faith life, and it can assist you in helping the younger members of our Church learn, grow, and live as active members of the Catholic community.

This resource can be used for private, family or communal prayer. The Order of Mass section incorporates the language of the revised Roman Missal.

Share the faith by giving copies of this book to others. In this way you are sharing in the ministry of our Lord, Jesus Christ, who called us to be his disciples and to share the Good News with all people.

Peace be with you,

RCL Benziger
RCLBenziger.com

CATHOLIC
PRAYERS AND PRACTICES
including THE ORDER OF MASS

The Sign of the Cross

In the name of the Father,
and of the Son,
and of the Holy Spirit. Amen.

Glory Be (Doxology)

Glory be to the Father
and to the Son
and to the Holy Spirit,
as it was in the beginning
is now, and ever shall be
world without end. Amen.

Our Father (Lord's Prayer)

Our Father, who art in heaven,
hallowed be thy name;
thy kingdom come,
thy will be done
on earth as it is in heaven.
Give us this day our daily
    bread,
and forgive us our trespasses,
as we forgive those who
    trespass against us;
and lead us not into
    temptation
    but deliver us from evil.
Amen.

Prayer to the Holy Spirit

Come, Holy Spirit, fill the
    hearts of your faithful.
And kindle in them the fire
    of your love.
Send forth your Spirit and
    they shall be created.
And you will renew the
    face of the earth.

The Hail Mary

Hail, Mary, full of grace,
the Lord is with thee.
Blessed art thou among
    women
and blessed is the fruit of thy
    womb, Jesus.
Holy Mary, Mother of God,
pray for us sinners,
now and at the hour of our
    death.
Amen.

Act of Contrition

My God,
I am sorry for my sins
   with all my heart.
In choosing to do wrong
and failing to do good,
I have sinned against you
whom I should love above all
   things.
I firmly intend, with your help,
to do penance,
to sin no more,
and to avoid whatever leads
   me to sin.
Our Savior Jesus Christ
suffered and died for us.
In his name, my God, have
   mercy.

Act of Faith

O my God, I firmly believe that
you are one God in three
divine Persons, Father, Son, and
Holy Spirit; I believe that your
divine Son became man and
died for our sins, and that he
will come to judge the living
and the dead. Amen.

Act of Hope

O my God,
relying on
your infinite
goodness and
promises, I
hope to obtain pardon of my
sins, the help of your grace,
and life everlasting, through
the merits of Jesus Christ, my
Lord and Redeemer.
Amen.

Act of Love

O my God, I love you above all
things, with my whole heart
and soul, because you are all
good and worthy of all my
love. I love my neighbor as
myself for the love of you.
I forgive all who have injured
me and I ask pardon of all
whom I have injured. Amen.

Nicene Creed

I believe in one God,
the Father almighty,
maker of heaven and earth,
of all things visible and
   invisible.

I believe in one Lord Jesus
   Christ,
the Only Begotten Son of God,
born of the Father before all
   ages.
God from God, Light from
   Light,
true God from true God,
begotten, not made,
   consubstantial with the
   Father;
through him all things were
   made.
For us men and for our
   salvation
he came down from heaven,
*(At the words that follow, up to and
including* and became man, *all
bow.)*

and by the Holy Spirit
   was incarnate of the
   Virgin Mary,
and became man.

For our sake he was crucified
   under Pontius Pilate,
he suffered death and was
   buried,

and rose again on the third day
in accordance with the
   Scriptures.
He ascended into heaven
and is seated at the right hand
   of the Father.
He will come again in glory
to judge the living and the
   dead
and his kingdom will have
   no end.

I believe in the Holy Spirit, the
   Lord, the giver of life,
who proceeds from the Father
   and the Son,
who with the Father and the
   Son is adored and glorified,
who has spoken through the
   prophets.

I believe in one, holy, catholic
   and apostolic Church.
I confess one Baptism
   for the forgiveness of sins
and I look forward to the
   resurrection of the dead
and the life of the world to
   come. Amen.

Apostles' Creed

I believe in God,
the Father almighty,
Creator of heaven and earth,
and in Jesus Christ,
    his only Son, our Lord,
*(At the words that follow, up to and
including* the Virgin Mary, *all bow.)*

who was conceived by the
    Holy Spirit,
born of the Virgin Mary,
suffered under Pontius Pilate,
was crucified, died and was
    buried;
he descended into hell;
on the third day he rose again
    from the dead;
he ascended into heaven,
and is seated at the right hand
    of God the Father almighty;
from there he will come to
    judge the living and the dead.

I believe in the Holy Spirit,
the holy catholic Church,
the communion of saints,
the forgiveness of sins,
the resurrection of the body,
and life everlasting. Amen.

Morning Prayer

Dear God,
as I begin this day,
keep me in your love and care.
Help me to live as your child
    today.
Bless me, my family,
    and my friends in all we do.
Keep us all close to you. Amen.

Evening Prayer

Dear God,
I thank you for today.
Keep me safe throughout
    the night.
Thank you for all the good
    I did today.
I am sorry for what I have
    chosen to do wrong.
Bless my family and friends.
    Amen.

A Vocation Prayer

God, I know you will call me
for special work in my life.
Help me follow Jesus each day
and be ready to answer
    your call.

Grace Before Meals

Bless us, O Lord,
and these thy gifts,
which we are about to receive
from thy bounty,
through Christ our Lord.
Amen.

The Divine Praises

Blessed be God.
Blessed be his holy name.
Blessed be Jesus Christ, true
God and true man.
Blessed be the name of Jesus.
Blessed be his most
Sacred Heart.
Blessed be his most precious
Blood.
Blessed be Jesus in the most
holy Sacrament of the altar.
Blessed be the Holy Spirit,
the Paraclete.
Blessed be the great Mother of
God, Mary most holy.
Blessed be her holy and
Immaculate Conception.
Blessed be her glorious
Assumption.
Blessed be the name of Mary,
Virgin and Mother.
Blessed be St. Joseph,
her most chaste spouse.
Blessed be God in his angels
and in his saints.

Grace After Meals

We give thee thanks,
for all thy benefits,
almighty God,
who lives and reigns forever.
Amen.

Prayer of Saint Francis

Lord, make me an instrument
of your peace:
where there is hatred,
let me sow love;
where there is injury, pardon;
where there is doubt, faith;
where there is despair, hope;
where there is darkness, light;
where there is sadness, joy.

O divine Master, grant that
I may not so much seek
to be consoled as to console,
to be understood as to
understand,
to be loved as
to love.
For it is in giving that
we receive,
it is in pardoning
that we are
pardoned,
it is in dying that
we are born to
eternal life.
Amen.

The Angelus

Leader: The Angel of the Lord declared unto Mary,

Response: and she conceived of the Holy Spirit.

All: Hail Mary . . .

Leader: Behold the handmaid of the Lord,

Response: Be it done unto me according to your Word.

All: Hail Mary . . .

Leader: And the Word was made flesh,

Response: And dwelt among us.

All: Hail Mary . . .

Leader: Pray for us, O Holy Mother of God,

Response: That we may be made worthy of the promises of Christ.

Leader: Let us pray.

Pour forth, we beseech you, oh Lord, your grace into our hearts; that we, to whom the Incarnation of Christ your Son was made known by the message of an Angel, may by his Passion and Cross be brought to the glory of his Resurrection. Through the same Christ our Lord.

All: Amen.

The Great Commandment

"You shall love the Lord, your God, with all your heart, with all your soul, and with all your mind. . . . You shall love your neighbor as yourself."

MATTHEW 22:37, 39

The New Commandment

[Jesus said:] "I give you a new commandment: love one another. As I have loved you, so you also should love one another. This is how all will know that you are my disciples, if you have love for one another."

JOHN 13:34-35

The Ten Commandments

1. I am the LORD your God: you shall not have strange gods before me.

2. You shall not take the name of the LORD your God in vain.

3. Remember to keep holy the LORD's Day.

4. Honor your father and your mother.

5. You shall not kill.

6. You shall not commit adultery.

7. You shall not steal.

8. You shall not bear false witness against your neighbor.

9. You shall not covet your neighbor's wife.

10. You shall not covet your neighbor's goods.

The Beatitudes

"Blessed are the poor in spirit,
for theirs is the kingdom of heaven.
Blessed are they who mourn,
for they will be comforted.
Blessed are the meek,
for they will inherit the land.
Blessed are they who hunger
and thirst for righteousness,
for they will be satisfied.
Blessed are the merciful,
for they will be shown mercy.
Blessed are the clean of heart,
for they will see God.
Blessed are the peacemakers,
for they will be called
children of God.
Blessed are they who are
persecuted for the sake of righteousness,
for theirs is the kingdom of heaven.
Blessed are you when they insult you and persecute you and utter every kind of evil against you [falsely] because of me. Rejoice and be glad, for your reward will be great in heaven."

MATTHEW 5:3-12

Corporal Works of Mercy

Feed people who are hungry.

Give drink to people who are thirsty.

Clothe people who need clothes.

Visit prisoners.

Shelter people who are homeless.

Visit people who are sick.

Bury people who have died.

Spiritual Works of Mercy

Help people who sin.

Teach people who are ignorant.

Give advice to people who have doubts.

Comfort people who suffer.

Be patient with other people.

Forgive people who hurt you.

Pray for people who are alive and for those who have died.

Gifts of the Holy Spirit

- Wisdom
- Understanding
- Right judgment (Counsel)
- Courage (Fortitude)
- Knowledge
- Reverence (Piety)
- Wonder and awe (Fear of the Lord)

Cardinal Virtues

- Prudence
- Justice
- Fortitude
- Temperance

Precepts of the Church

1. Participate in Mass on Sundays and holy days of obligation and rest from unnecessary work.

2. Confess sins at least once a year.

3. Receive Holy Communion at least during the Easter season.

4. Observe the prescribed days of fasting and abstinence.

5. Provide for the material needs of the Church, each according to one's abilities.

We pray the
ROSARY

5 Pray the Hail, Holy Queen. Make the Sign of the Cross.

3 Think of the first mystery. Pray an Our Father, 10 Hail Marys, and the Glory Be.

4 Repeat step 3 for each of the next 4 mysteries.

2 Pray an Our Father, 3 Hail Marys and the Glory Be.

1 Make the Sign of the Cross and pray the Apostles' Creed.

Rosary

Catholics pray the Rosary to honor Mary and remember the important events in the lives of Jesus and Mary. There are twenty mysteries of the Rosary. Follow the steps from 1 to 5.

Joyful Mysteries

1. The Annunciation
2. The Visitation
3. The Nativity
4. The Presentation in the Temple
5. The Finding of the Child Jesus After Three Days in the Temple

Luminous Mysteries

1. The Baptism at the Jordan
2. The Miracle at Cana
3. The Proclamation of the Kingdom and the Call to Conversion
4. The Transfiguration
5. The Institution of the Eucharist

Sorrowful Mysteries

1. The Agony in the Garden
2. The Scourging at the Pillar
3. The Crowning with Thorns
4. The Carrying of the Cross
5. The Crucifixion and Death

Glorious Mysteries

1. The Resurrection
2. The Ascension
3. The Descent of the Holy Spirit at Pentecost
4. The Assumption of Mary
5. The Crowning of the Blessed Virgin as Queen of Heaven and Earth

Hail, Holy Queen

Hail, holy Queen, Mother of mercy:
Hail, our life, our sweetness and our hope.

To you do we cry, poor banished children of Eve. To you do we send up our sighs, mourning and weeping in this valley of tears.
Turn then, most gracious advocate,
your eyes of mercy toward us;
and after this our exile
show unto us the blessed fruit of your womb, Jesus.
O clement, O loving, O sweet Virgin Mary.

Stations of the Cross

1. Jesus is condemned to death.
2. Jesus accepts his cross.
3. Jesus falls the first time.
4. Jesus meets his mother.
5. Simon helps Jesus carry the cross.
6. Veronica wipes the face of Jesus.
7. Jesus falls the second time.
8. Jesus meets the women.
9. Jesus falls the third time.
10. Jesus is stripped of his clothes.
11. Jesus is nailed to the cross.
12. Jesus dies on the cross.
13. Jesus is taken down from the cross.
14. Jesus is buried in the tomb.

Some parishes conclude the Stations by reflecting on the Resurrection of Jesus.

CATHOLIC SOCIAL TEACHING

The Church's teaching on social justice guides us in living lives of holiness and building a just society. These principles are:

1. All human life is sacred. The basic equality of all people flows from their dignity as human persons and the rights that flow from that dignity.

2. The human person is the principle, the object, and the subject of every social group.

3. The human person has been created by God to belong to and to participate in a family and other social communities.

4. Respect for the rights of people flows from their dignity as persons. Society and all social organizations must promote virtue and protect human life and human rights and guarantee the conditions that promote the exercise of freedom.

5. Political communities and public authority are based on human nature. They belong to an order established by God.

6. All human authority must be used for the common good of society.

7. The common good of society consists of respect for and promotion of the fundamental rights of the human person; the just development of material and spiritual goods of society; and the peace and safety of all people.

8. We need to work to eliminate the sinful inequalities that exist between peoples and for the improvement of the living conditions of people. The needs of the poor and vulnerable have a priority.

9. We are one human and global family. We are to share our spiritual blessings, even more than our material blessings.

Based on the *Catechism of the Catholic Church*

SIGNS AND SYMBOLS
of the CATHOLIC CHURCH

From its beginning the Church used signs and symbols to help us profess our faith. These symbols unite us. They help us understand what Catholics believe.

Paschal Candle

The Paschal candle, also called the Easter candle, is a symbol of the Risen Christ who is the Light of the world.

Cross

The Cross is one of the most widely used symbols of our faith. It reminds us that Jesus died on the Cross and was raised from the dead. A crucifix is a Cross with Jesus' body fixed to it.

Alpha and Omega

Alpha and Omega are the first and last letters of the Greek alphabet. They remind us that Jesus is the beginning and end of everything that is.

Chi-Rho

The Chi-Rho is a symbol for Christ. It comes from the first two letters of the Greek word for Christ.

The Good Shepherd

Jesus is often represented as the Good Shepherd who leads and cares for his sheep. The sheep symbolize those who follow Christ.

THE SEVEN SACRAMENTS

Jesus gave the Church the Seven Sacraments. The Sacraments are the main liturgical signs of the Church. They make the Paschal Mystery of Jesus, who is always the main celebrant of each Sacrament, present to us. They make us sharers in the saving work of Christ and in the life of the Holy Trinity.

SACRAMENTS OF INITIATION

Baptism
Through Baptism we are joined to Christ and become members of the Body of Christ, the Church. We are reborn as adopted children of God the Father and receive the gift of the Holy Spirit. Original Sin and all personal sins are forgiven.

Confirmation
Confirmation completes Baptism. In this Sacrament the gift of the Holy Spirit strengthens us to live our Baptism.

Eucharist
Sharing in the Eucharist joins us most fully to Christ and to the Church. We share in the one sacrifice of Christ. The bread and wine become the Body and Blood of Christ through the power of the Holy Spirit and the words of the priest. We receive the Body and Blood of Christ.

SACRAMENTS OF HEALING

Penance and Reconciliation
Through the ministry of the priest we receive forgiveness of sins committed after our Baptism. We need to confess all mortal sins.

Anointing of the Sick
Anointing of the Sick strengthens our faith and trust in God when we are seriously ill, dying, or weak because of old age.

SACRAMENTS AT THE SERVICE OF COMMUNION

Holy Orders

Through Holy Orders a baptized man is consecrated to serve the whole Church as a bishop, priest, or deacon in the name of Christ. Bishops, who are the successors of the Apostles, receive this Sacrament most fully. They are consecrated to teach the Gospel, to lead the Church in the worship of God, and to guide the Church to live holy lives. Bishops are helped by priests, their coworkers, and by deacons in their work.

Matrimony

Matrimony unites a baptized man and a baptized woman in a lifelong bond of faithful love to always honor each other and to accept the gift of children from God. In this Sacrament the married couple is consecrated to be a sign of Christ's love for the Church.

The RITE of PENANCE AND RECONCILIATION

Individual Rite

- Greeting
- Scripture Reading
- Confession of Sins and Acceptance of Penance
- Act of Contrition
- Absolution
- Closing Prayer

Communal Rite

- Greeting
- Scripture Reading
- Homily
- Examination of Conscience with a litany of contrition and the Lord's Prayer
- Individual Confession and Absolution
- Closing Prayer

WE CELEBRATE THE MASS

The INTRODUCTORY RITES

We remember that we are the community of the Church. We prepare to listen to the Word of God and to celebrate the Eucharist.

The Entrance

We stand as the priest approaches the altar with the deacon, and other ministers. We sing a gathering song. The priest and deacon kiss the altar. The priest then goes to the chair where he presides over the celebration.

Sign of the Cross and Greeting

The priest leads us in praying the Sign of the Cross. The priest greets us, and we say, **"And with your spirit."**

The Penitential Act

We admit our wrongdoings. We bless God for his mercy.

Gloria

Glory to God in the highest, and on earth peace to people of good will.

We praise you,
we bless you,
we adore you,
we glorify you,
we give you thanks for your
     great glory,
Lord God, heavenly King,
O God, almighty Father.

Lord Jesus Christ, Only
     Begotten Son,
Lord God, Lamb of God, Son
     of the Father,
you take away the sins of
     the world,
  have mercy on us;
you take away the sins of
     the world,
  receive our prayer;
you are seated at the right
     hand of the Father,
  have mercy on us.

For you alone are the Holy One,
you alone are the Lord,
you alone are the Most High,
Jesus Christ,
with the Holy Spirit,
in the glory of God the Father.
Amen.

The Collect
The priest leads us in praying the Collect. We respond, **"Amen."**

The LITURGY of the WORD

God speaks to us today. We listen and respond to God's Word.

The First Reading
We sit and listen as the reader reads from the Old Testament or from the Acts of the Apostles. The reader concludes, **"The word of the Lord."** We respond, **"Thanks be to God."**

The Responsorial Psalm
The cantor leads us in singing a psalm.

The Second Reading
The reader reads from the New Testament, but not from the four Gospels. The reader concludes, **"The word of the Lord."** We respond, **"Thanks be to God."**

Acclamation
We stand to honor Christ present with us in the Gospel. The cantor leads us in singing **"Alleluia, Alleluia, Alleluia"** or another chant during Lent.

The Gospel
The deacon or priest proclaims, "A reading from the holy Gospel according to (name of Gospel writer)." We respond, **"Glory to you, O Lord."** He proclaims the Gospel. At the end, he says, "The Gospel of the Lord." We respond, **"Praise to you, Lord Jesus Christ."**

The Homily
We sit. The priest or deacon preaches the homily. He helps the whole community understand the Word of God spoken to us in the readings.

The Profession of Faith
We stand and profess our faith. We pray the Nicene Creed together.

Nicene Creed

I believe in one God,
the Father almighty,
maker of heaven and earth,
of all things visible and
    invisible.

I believe in one Lord Jesus
    Christ,
the Only Begotten Son of God,
born of the Father before all
    ages.
God from God, Light from
    Light,
true God from true God,
begotten, not made,
    consubstantial with the
    Father;
through him all things were
    made.
For us men and for our
    salvation
he came down from heaven,
(At the words that follow, up to and
including and became man, *all*
bow.)

and by the Holy Spirit
    was incarnate of the
    Virgin Mary,
and became man.

For our sake he was crucified
    under Pontius Pilate,
he suffered death and was
    buried,

and rose again on the third day
in accordance with the
    Scriptures.
He ascended into heaven
and is seated at the right hand
    of the Father.
He will come again in glory
to judge the living and the
    dead
and his kingdom will have
    no end.

I believe in the Holy Spirit, the
    Lord, the giver of life,
who proceeds from the Father
    and the Son,
who with the Father and the
    Son is adored and glorified,
who has spoken through the
    prophets.

I believe in one, holy, catholic
    and apostolic Church.
I confess one Baptism
    for the forgiveness of sins
and I look forward to the
    resurrection of the dead
and the life of the world to
    come. Amen.

Instead of the Niceno-
Constantinopolitan Creed,
especially during Lent and and
Easter Time, the baptismal Symbol
of the Roman Church, known as
the Apostles' Creed, may be used.

Apostles' Creed

I believe in God,
the Father almighty,
Creator of heaven and earth,
and in Jesus Christ,
  his only Son, our Lord,
*(At the words that follow, up to and
including* the Virgin Mary, *all bow.)*

who was conceived by the
  Holy Spirit,
born of the Virgin Mary,
suffered under Pontius Pilate,
was crucified, died and was
  buried;
he descended into hell;
on the third day he rose again
  from the dead;
he ascended into heaven,
and is seated at the right hand
  of God the Father almighty;
from there he will come to
  judge the living and the dead.

I believe in the Holy Spirit,
the holy catholic Church,
the communion of saints,
the forgiveness of sins,
the resurrection of the body,
and life everlasting. Amen.

The Prayer of the Faithful

The priest leads us in praying
for our Church and its leaders,
for our country and its leaders,
for ourselves and others, for the
sick and those who have died.

We can respond to each prayer
in several ways. One way we
respond is, **"Lord, hear our
prayer."**

The LITURGY of the EUCHARIST

*We join with Jesus and the Holy
Spirit to give thanks and praise to
God the Father.*

The Preparation of the Altar and Gifts

We sit as the altar is prepared
and the collection is taken up.
We share our blessings with
the community of the Church
and especially with those in
need. The cantor may lead us
in singing a song. The gifts of
bread and wine are brought
to the altar.

The priest lifts up the bread
and blesses God for all our
gifts. He prays, "Blessed are you,
Lord God of all creation, . . ."
We respond, **"Blessed be
God for ever."**

The priest lifts up the cup of wine and prays, "Blessed are you, Lord God of all creation, . . ." We respond, **"Blessed be God for ever."**

The priest invites us, "Pray, brethren (brothers and sisters), that my sacrifice and yours may be acceptable to God, the almighty Father."

We stand and respond, **"May the Lord accept the sacrifice at your hands for the praise and glory of his name, for our good and the good of all his holy Church."**

The Prayer over the Offerings

The priest leads us in praying the Prayer over the Offerings. We respond, **"Amen."**

Preface

The priest invites us to join in praying the Church's great prayer of praise and thanksgiving to God the Father.

Priest: "The Lord be with you."
Assembly: "And with your spirit."
Priest: "Lift up your hearts."

Assembly: "We lift them up to the Lord."
Priest: "Let us give thanks to the Lord our God."
Assembly: "It is right and just."

After the priest sings or prays aloud the Preface, we acclaim, **"Holy, Holy, Holy Lord God of hosts. Heaven and earth are full of your glory. Hosanna in the highest. Blessed is he who comes in the name of the Lord. Hosanna in the highest."**

The Eucharistic Prayer

The priest leads the assembly in praying the Eucharistic Prayer. We call upon the Holy Spirit to make our gifts of bread and wine holy and that they become the Body and Blood of Jesus. We recall what happened at the Last Supper. The bread and wine become the Body and Blood of the Lord.

Jesus is truly and really present under the appearances of bread and wine. The priest sings or says aloud, "The mystery of faith." We respond using this or another acclamation used by the Church,

"We proclaim your Death, O Lord, and profess your Resurrection until you come again."

The priest then prays for the Church. He prays for the living and the dead.

Doxology

The priest concludes the praying of the Eucharistic Prayer. He sings or prays aloud, "Through him, and with him, and in him,
O God, almighty Father, in the unity of the Holy Spirit, all glory and honor is yours, for ever and ever."
We respond, **"Amen."**

The COMMUNION RITE

The Lord's Prayer
We pray the Lord's Prayer.

The Sign of Peace
The priest invites us to share a sign of peace, saying, "The peace of the Lord be with you always." We respond, **"And with your spirit."** We share a sign of peace.

The Fraction, or the Breaking of the Bread
The priest breaks the host, the consecrated bread. We sing or pray aloud,

**"Lamb of God, you take away the sins of the world, have mercy on us.
Lamb of God, you take away the sins of the world, have mercy on us.
Lamb of God, you take away the sins of the world, grant us peace."**

Communion
The priest raises the host and says aloud, "Behold the Lamb of God, behold him who takes away the sins of the world. Blessed are those called to the supper of the Lamb."

We join with him and say, **"Lord, I am not worthy that you should enter under my roof, but only say the word and my soul shall be healed."**

The priest receives Communion. Next, the deacon, the extraordinary ministers of Holy Communion, and the members of the assembly receive Communion.

The priest, deacon, or extraordinary minister of Holy Communion holds up the host. We bow and the priest, deacon, or extraordinary minister of Holy Communion says, "The Body of Christ." We respond, **"Amen."** We then receive the consecrated host in our hand or on our tongue.

If we are to receive the Blood of Christ, the priest, deacon, or extraordinary minister of Holy Communion holds up the cup containing the consecrated wine. We bow and the priest, deacon, or extraordinary minister of Holy Communion says, "The Blood of Christ." We respond, **"Amen."** We take the cup in our hands and drink from it.

The Prayer after Communion
We stand as the priest invites us to pray, saying, "Let us pray." He prays the Prayer after Communion. We respond, **"Amen."**

The CONCLUDING RITES

We are sent forth to do good works, praising and blessing the Lord.

Greeting
We stand. The priest greets us as we prepare to leave. He says, "The Lord be with you." We respond, **"And with your spirit."**

Blessing
The priest or deacon may invite us, "Bow down for the blessing." The priest blesses us, saying, "May almighty God bless you, the Father, and the Son, and the Holy Spirit." We respond, **"Amen."**

Dismissal of the People
The priest or deacon sends us forth, using these or similar words, "Go and announce the Gospel of the Lord." We respond, **"Thanks be to God."**

We sing a hymn. The priest and the deacon kiss the altar. The priest, deacon, and other ministers bow to the altar and leave in procession.